D1569286

Colorado
Trout Fishing
Methods and Techniques

Second Edition

1   2   3   4   5   6   7   8   9

Printed in the United States of America

ISBN 0-9617325-2-0

Merton D. Leeper
11151 W. 27th Place
Lakewood, CO 80215

Designed and Typeset by:

Talbot House Publication Services
4680 Talbot Drive
Boulder, CO 80303

Cover Design by:
Robert F. Wilson

I wish to dedicate this book to my wife, Mary, who has supported me in my every endeavor. Not only are you my best friend and lover, you are quite a fisherlady! There was never an M&M Connection like us. I also wish to dedicate this book to my children, Talli and Cecily, who know intimately how dedicated I am to the "Art of Fishing."

Introduction

Have you ever heard the statement that 10 percent of the fishermen catch 90 percent of the fish? Or have you ever gone to a lake or a river and noticed one person that was consistently catching fish even though no one else did? The intent of this book is to provide and arm the reader with enough information that he/she can be confident that on any fishing trip, under any conditions, fish will be caught.

Since before I could walk I've always had a fascination with aquatic life via a small aquarium in my room. At about age six, my father began to talk to me about when he would begin taking me fishing with him. He began by telling me that fishing took patience—and when he thought I had the required amount he would then take me. In the meantime, upon his return home from his excursions, he would always save a couple of fish for me to clean. At the brisk age of eight, I was an expert fish cleaner, even though I'd never yet been fishing . . . but this was my year. Dad began taking me to his denizens of the deep and allowing me to reel his fish in as he caught them.

At age ten, I graduated into a full fledged fisherperson with my own pole, reel, tackle box and boots. This was the year I caught my first fish independently— putting on my own hook and bait, as well as casting to the fish.

These trout were first introduced to this state in the 1880s. They are known for their great jumping abilities and are the primary trout caught in Colorado. *Salmo gairdneri* is a willing foe, likely to be caught by any of the fishing means described in this text. The Colorado state record of 18 pounds 5 ounces was caught in the South Platte River in 1972. The ideal water temperature, when this fish is most active, is 55 degrees. Past records for this species, outside Colorado, include a 37-pounder caught in Lake Pend Oreille, Idaho in 1947. The rainbow is a spring spawner.

CUTTHROAT TROUT *Salmo clarki*

small, irregularly shaped black spots, sparse on belly

cutthroat slash—one on each side
(weak on juveniles)

spots more dense toward rear of fish

This is the only true trout native to Colorado, it is still found in many lakes and streams but is not usually caught in its true native form. This is due to the introduction of the rainbow trout which also spawns in the spring. These two species have hybridized to a degree in waterways in which they share together. They are not as easily caught as the rainbow, this is probably due to the lesser numbers of them. The Colorado state record is 16 pounds, caught in Twin Lakes in 1964. Past records, outside Colorado, include a 41-pounder caught in Pyramid Lake, Nevada in 1925. The ideal water temperature for this species is 55 degrees.

GOLDEN TROUT *Salmo aquabonita*

round black spots
on upper 1/3 of body

numerous spots on
dorsal fin and tail

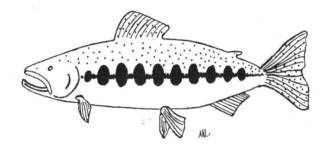

lower side
yellow to golden

10-12 parr marks
(may persist on adults)

about 200 scales
in lateral line

To catch a golden trout in one's lifetime is an honorable endeavor. This trout is found in only a few high mountain lakes in alpine settings, usually above 10,000 feet in elevation. It was introduced in Colorado in 1932, from the State of Wyoming. The golden trout is a California native trout. Their numbers are few, the largest recorded in Colorado weighed 3 pounds 10 ounces, it was caught at Kelly Lake in 1979. The golden is a spring spawner.

LAKE TROUT *Salvelinus namaycush*

numerous light spots,
none red or orange

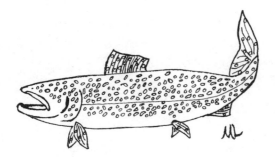

white leading edge often present on fins

tail deeply forked,
shortest ray less than
1/2 length of longest

This trout often known as the Mackinaw, is the largest of the trout species, it seeks the coldest and deepest waters of all trout. This original "Big Mac" is mostly caught in the spring and fall months on trolling gear and from the banks of large impoundments using sucker meat as bait. Twenty-plus-pounders are not uncommon in this state. A 40-pound specimen was gill netted, tagged, filmed, and released back into Granby Reservoir in 1988. The Colorado state record is a 36-pounder caught in Deep Lake in 1949. Past records for this species, outside Colorado, include a 65-pounder caught in Great Bear Lake, Northwest territories, in 1970. The lake trout is a spring spawner, its ideal water temperature is 50 degrees.

PACIFIC SOCKEYE SALMON *Oncorhynchus nerka*

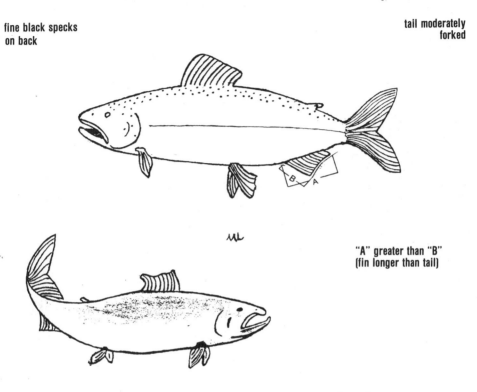

adipose fin

fine black specks
on back

tail moderately
forked

"A" greater than "B"
(fin longer than tail)

spawning male

Known in Colorado as the kokanee salmon, this salmon was first introduced into this state in 1951. It is a land-locked variety that was transplanted from the Pacific sockeye salmon strain. It is primarily caught by two legal methods, angling and snagging. In the fall when these salmon spawn, it is not uncommon to snag the current legal limit of forty fish in just a few hours. This variety of salmon dies after its four-year spawning cycle. The Colorado state record for angling is 6 pounds 13 ounces. It was caught in September 1986 in Spinney Mountain Reservoir, while the record for snagging is 6 pounds 3 ounces, caught in 1978 at Eleven Mile Reservoir.

Equipment

January is a good time to sit down in front of a cozy fireplace and dig out all your equipment to make sure that it's ready at a moments notice. If you have new equipment, this is not so important, but if your equipment is a season or more old, then you need to focus in on some specific areas.

The following text will identify wear areas on rods and reels that are readily discernable, disclose internal wear areas on open- and closed-faced reels, show you a method to easily start a new line upon the reel spool where no trailing ends have to be clipped, and a blow-by-blow description of how to professionally wrap rod guides.

FISHING RODS

It's exciting to be living in a modern age of technology and confusing too. For instance, when purchasing a new rod, should I get graphite, boron, or a glass rod? Boron material is the thinnest and most sensitive, followed by graphite, and then fiberglass. I would recommend that you select, for trout fishing, a rod of six to six and one-half feet in length that feels good to you, irregardless of its make up. I have a collection of all the above types of rods and feel that each has its own

F.

Pull with pliars

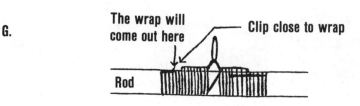

Rod

Put the guide wrapping material through the loop you have created and pull the two loose ends with pliars and you will pull the wrapping material back through itself—and voila, you have a professional guide wrap with no apparent beginning or end.

G.

The wrap will come out here — Clip close to wrap

Rod

Put on a color wrap stabilizer, schellac, and you have just saved yourself several dollars.

REELS

Now with your rod in A-1 shape, it's time to focus on your reel. Even though you may not be mechanically inclined, believe me, they are as simple as putting a new cartridge into a ball point pen.

Reels for trout fishing generally come in two types, the open-faced reel and the closed-faced reel.

Open-Faced Reels

These reels are probably the most maintenance free of any, but they do need maintenance similar to the checks on your rod. The main wear area that must be checked carefully for grooves or deterioration is where the line crosses the bail. On most open-faced reels, this piece is replaceable and easy to get from the manufacturer or reel repair shops. This area of wear is the second area to check (the first being your rod guides) when you are having line breakage problems. The diagram below will illustrate the area of wear and the repair.

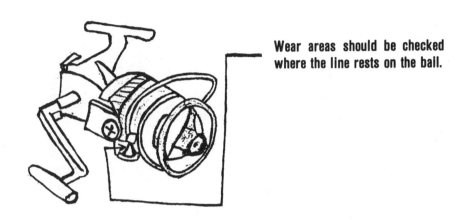

Wear areas should be checked where the line rests on the bail.

Closed-Faced Reels

Closed-faced reels seem to be more complex and difficult to repair because one must remove parts to make these repairs. An example of a typical problem is as follows. On a recent fishing trip, I had caught and released several trout until my line began to break about every third cast. The rod was new and my line had just been changed, so I knew that the problem was in the reel. As I sat upon the bank investigating the reel, I noticed that at the cap the line had grooved the metal to a small degree (problem #1)—upon removing the cap and investigating the works, I noticed another groove directly in front of the ceramic pickup pin where the line

You may choose to change the line altogether, in which case, a new problem arises. How to attach the new line to the spool. I have often seen people tie knots on the spool, then clip off the end, inside the spool with a knife—possibly grooving the spool itself. Here is an excellent method to use that won't damage your spool.

A.

Spool

Tie a slip knot first, then tie an overhand knot on the terminal end of the line

B.

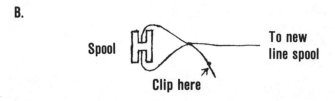

Spool

To new line spool

Clip here

Put slip knot over spool, clip this end outside of the reel, pull tight and you are ready to reel on your new line.

18

THE TACKLE BOX

Now for the tackle box, what minimal amount of equipment is needed for all types of trout fishing? Hooks are a good place to start. I prefer sizes 6, 8, and 10, some bell-shaped sinkers, a jar of salmon eggs, swivels, some lures, flies, bubbles (floats), two stringers for all the fish, and a net.

Snelled hooks are generally quite reasonable to buy, but you can professionally snell your own and save even more, this is how:

A.

Select your hook. Cut about an eight-inch section of monofilament.

B.

One terminal end of the section of monofilament goes through the eye downward, while the other goes through upward. The longest length of line is above the eye.

C.

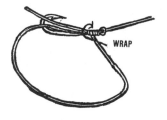

Hold with your forefinger and thumb both pieces of monofilament against the shank of the hook. Next, take the line that makes the loop and begin to wrap it around the shank (from the eye down).

Below are several diagrams that show the water conditions and trout movements throughout the seasons.

Midsummer

Surface _____ 70°

Epilimnion **Highly Oxygenated but warm**

_____ 60°

Oxygenated but cold temps

Brown 60°
Cutthroat &
Rainbow 55°
Thermocline **Brook 54°**
Mackinaw 50°

_____ 50°

Oxygen only in upper portion of this layer
Hypolimnion

_____ 39°

In midsummer, the trout are most active in the thermocline layer where their ideal water temperatures generally exist. Mackinaw or lake trout are suspended in the upper layers of the hypolimnion or lower layers of the thermocline. Late summer further forces this fish upward to higher temperatures than are ideal because the hypolimnion layer has become stagnant and little oxygen is left.

Early Fall

Surface_____68°

Epilimnion   Highly oxygenated-still warm

                                                  Brown   62°
          _____
                                                  Rainbow & 55°
                                                  Cutthroat
                                                  Brook 54°
Thermocline   Oxygenated & cold   Mackinaw 52°
          _____50°
Hypolimnion

                    Stagnant & devoid of oxygen

          _____39°

In the early fall, the various species of trout are forced into the two upper layers of water because of the lack of oxygen in the bottom layer. Note that the brown trout and Mackinaw are now in a water level above the midsummer level and in a temperature a couple of degrees above their ideal temperature.

Fall Turnover

Surface_____39°

                              Rainbow

Epilimnion   Brook   Mackinaw

                    Warmer surface layers of water
                    replace the sinking surface water.
          Brown   All water highly oxygenated.

                              Cutthroat
Hypolimnion _____39°

As the cool breezes and temperatures of winter approach, the surface water cools down to thirty-nine degrees. At thirty-nine degrees, water sinks. As it sinks, it takes with it the highly oxygenated surface water to the bottom. The subsurface warmer layers of water then replace the surface water, are cooled to thirty-nine degrees and then sink to the bottom. This process continues until both the epilimnion and hypolimnion layers of water are oxygen rich. Eventually, the water from top to bottom is thirty-nine degrees. The thermocline layer of water at this time ceases to exist.

To the trout fisherman, this is the time of the year that all trout species can be caught from the surface waters to the bottom. Before the completion of the fall turnover, the fish are especially active, this is because the subsurface water temperature is variable as the sinking surface water mixes with it. Eventually, as early winter approaches, the water is thirty-nine degrees from top to bottom and the trout become sluggish and lethargic because they are existing at temperatures below the ideal.

Early Winter

Surface Ice_____30°

Epilimnion   Oxygen rich but very cold
                    _____36°

Hypolimnion   Warmer temperatures &
                oxygen rich from fall turnover

                All trout in this layer   39°

Early winter waters differ from late winter water in the following way. At first, the early winter fish can be found in the warmer lower levels of the water. As late

24

winter approaches (below), the oxygen in the lower layer begins to deteriorate and forces the fish into the cooler upper layers. If the oxygen completely deteriorates in a lake, the result is winterkill.

Late Winter

Surface Ice		30°
Epilimnion	Oxygen exists but very cold	
	All trout in this layer	36°
Hypolimnion		
	Devoid of oxygen	39°

As you can see, winter fishing really differs! Early winter anglers fish the lower bottom layers of the water, while the late winter angler should be fishing a short distance below the surface.

Early Spring

Surface		34°
	Oxygen rich cool layer	
Epilimnion		
	All trout species suspended here	
Hypolimnion	Devoid of oxygen.	39°

The ice cover is melting, significantly oxygenating the epilimnion layer. This layer is still very cool, thus, the suspended trout are sluggish. Very soon, after ice out, the surface water begins to warm. At thirty-nine degrees, the oxygen-rich surface water begins to sink. This is the start of the spring turnover.

Spring Turnover

Surface _____ 39°

Epilimnion   Highly oxygenated surface water
              sinks to oxygenate the water from
              top to bottom. Trout are
              everywhere.

Hypolimnion _____ 39°

As the surface warms to thirty-nine degrees, it begins to sink, being replaced by cooler subsurface water, which is heated to thirty-nine degrees and then sinks. At this time the trout are dispersed from top to bottom.

Early Summer

Surface _____ 65°

Epilimnion   Highly Oxygenated

_____ Brown 60°
                        Cutthroat & Rainbow 55°
Thermocline
                   Highly Oxygenated   Brook 54°

_____ 52°
                                    Mackinaw 50°
Hypolimnion   Highly Oxygenated

_____ 39°

Understanding water phenomena, temperature impacts on the water, and fish movement will allow you to better estimate where the fish are during any season. In the balmy warm months of the year, you can now clearly understand why the fish surface in the evening and morning hours. It is likely, in a lake like Dillon Reservoir, that as the evening waters cool, sometimes after dark, the brown trout become extremely active on the surface (which has cooled to their sixty degree ideal water temperature). Likewise, as the waters continue to cool throughout the night and early morning hours, the rainbow and cutthroat trout become active and hit the surface which has cooled to their fifty-five degree ideal temperature.

More and more fisherman have begun utilizing weighted temperature devices attached to a line, measured every ten yards, to accurately locate the ideal water temperature of the species they are seeking and the exact depth. This is usually done from a boat or a drop off at the lakes edge. Another method to determine the temperature of the water you are fishing in is this. You will need a glass thermometer (the pet store aquarium variety will do fine). Then you must catch a trout—look around to see that no one is watching (they will think you have gone over the deep end). Take your thermometer out of your pocket and push it into the fishes mouth and gullet . . .the temperature of the trout is the temperature of the water it was caught in.

4

Bait Fishing

Introduction

From a very early age, I was interested in the out-of-doors, especially in night crawlers. What neat creatures! They didn't even seem to mind my stretching, tugging, or even the comfort of my pocket. I used to pick these critters for my Dad before he went fishing and would pride myself in his catch because I had a part in it. My father kept telling me that fishing took patience and work and that he would take me fishing only when my attention span exceeded two or three minutes. At age ten, my Dad arrived home from work and informed me that opening day of the fishing season was that weekend and I was invited. My first real fishing trip—wow, was I excited!

We were bound for Corona Pass in Colorado and would walk into one of several lakes in the area. I was in seventh heaven but really couldn't understand all the lugging around of ice boxes, stoves, sleeping bags, extra clothes and so forth that we were taking. Off we went to pick up Dad's fishing friend John Churchy, who was himself a real outdoorsman and a good fisherman. I knew I was in good company and hoped their luck would rub off on me.

As we drove through the mountains, I marveled at the scenery. The deep green of the pine trees and the contrasting aspen which were just beginning to leaf out gave way to an eerie looking tundra as we went above timberline. It was at this point, that I first noticed the cold. Kind of like placing your hand into an ice box but not wanting to leave it there. I was daydreaming about my first fishing trip when I heard Dad say, "Roll up the window, it's freezing out there!" Almost immediately after he said this, we abruptly stopped, in fact, the road had disappeared around a bend and was totally engulfed in snow.

After a couple of very cold hours of winching our four-wheeled "woody" to a place clear of snow, Dad and John got very excited and talked about the large fish that inhabited some mystical lake that I couldn't even see. I envisioned a lake free of ice and snow next to the road where I could come and go from the lake to the comfort of our vehicle. My bubble was about to break.

As Dad and John began to put layers and layers of clothing on, the thought hit me that I could freeze out there! So, I began to layer my clothing, adding a candy bar here and there for nourishment. One thought puzzled me though, how was I going to keep my feet warm? Dad had just that week bought me some Pack-type boots, but I thought they were to be used when I grew up more . . . they were at least ten sizes to big for me. As I opened up the shiney new box where my oversize boots were, I saw four pairs of heavy wool socks and saw my feet grow before me from one layer to another. I was surprised to find that my boots fit perfectly. I was at last ready to trek through this unfamiliar wilderness.

I can remember several times asking them to slow up. It seemed that three of my steps equalled their one and that my new clothes weighed a ton. Also, I could not get used to walking in those huge boots and often tripped myself only to fall into the snow. I think Dad was frustrated because he and John kept looking at me and saying, "Hurry up, or it'll be dark before we reach the lake." Shucks, it was just light and if it was that far, I knew I was in trouble.

At last, we walked down into a steep valley where the snow gave way to a crystal clear lake. I can clearly remember a real feeling of accomplishment as I sat upon a large flat rock next to this magnificent lake. Dad told me to stay here and he and John would stay within shouting distance as they fished around the lake.

So here I was, on this cold hard rock, fishing pole in hand and wondering if it was worth it all. But I was determined to show Dad and John that they made the right decision to take me along. I knew how to make knots, they were my specialty, so I got a hook out of my very own shiney new tackle box and tied it on with a square knot. Next, I tied a sinker to the line and took a big night crawler out of my pocket and with much difficulty impailed it on the hook. Now what? I had a problem. I knew how the reel worked, but really didn't have the hang of it. Three casts later and three night crawlers later, I realized that my Dad's careful instruction on "How to cast" was not working well at all and I was really cold too.

As I sat on my rock and looked into the lake dejectedly, my eyes caught movement. As I focused, I realized I could actually see fish. Now my determination to catch one soared. I rebaited my hook, sat for a moment to figure out just how I was going to get my line into the water and—zingo—an idea hit me. I knew how to release the line and how to reel it in, but I just couldn't cast. So, I pulled about twelve yards of line out of the reel and spread it out carefully behind me, took the weight in hand and gave it my best fast ball . . . to my surprise, all the line went out and I was fishing.

Almost immediately, my rod came alive. I yelled at the top of my lungs, "I gotta bite, Dad. I gotta bite" and grabbed my pole and began to reel in. I wanted that fish so bad that it seemed like ages had passed before it came in to the bank and airplaned it over my head onto a snow bank. I grabbed it like a coyote that hadn't eaten in weeks and proudly let everyone know within a mile that "I caught one, I caught one!" By the end of the day, I had four fish, a big ego, and a lot of confidence in myself. That hike back up the valley was something else though! I think that I stopped every ten feet, but it was somehow different now because Dad and John could see in me how special this outing was and what it meant to me. Even though I was freezing to death when we finally got to our Willy's, my first question was, "Dad, when can we go fishing again?" And I have never lost my enthusiasm since that first trip.

This was my introduction to the art of fishing with bait. The following section is meant to hone your skills, increase your creel take, and bring to light some unique ways to fish with bait.

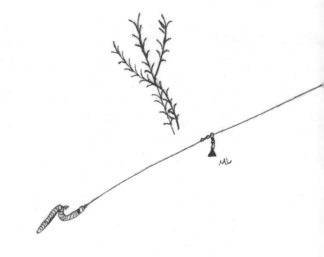

Many fishermen call themselves purists and refuse to fish with anything but flies and lures, others fish only with baits. I am in the middle of the road (Colorado allows the use of two rods, with the purchase of a second Rod Stamp) utilizing one rod with bait and the other with flies or lures. Bait fishing for trout in Colorado probably creels more fish than any other means and it does take a certain amount of skill.

This skill is in the form of identifying potential productive areas of a lake or stream and then to present your bait in such a way as to attract strikes. Sounds easy, but I assure you it's not. Some areas are always productive while others are not. Good bets are rocky coves and inlets in lakes, and ripples proceeding pools in rivers.

There is a small controversy among bait fishermen regarding the various ways to rig up for trout. The two most common are to either place your weight (A) about two feet above your line or to place it on the terminal end of the line (B).

A.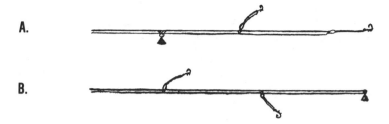

B.

There are some advantages to both. In (B), when fishing fairly deep water full of vegetation, the sinker is grounded on the bottom allowing the bait to rest above the vegetation (if you use a light line). In (A), the bait is presented first and rests directly on the bottom awaiting a big fat trout to come along.

The best method is (C), where a swivel without a snap and a swivel with a snap is used in conjunction with a bell weight, leader and appropriate hooks. It looks like this:

C.

This method is the best and unfortunately is the most time consuming to prepare. This setup allows the line to freewheel through the swivel and thus when a strike occurs there is a little drag. If you are fishing for lake trout, this setup makes the difference between catching and losing a wary lunker.

I generally use method (C) because I have simply had better luck with it. Try using a good proven brand of salmon eggs on a #10 hook, fill the hook up with three to four eggs and cast it out. Try one pole out as far as you can reach and the other only a few yards from shore. I have seen it when all the fishing was twenty feet from the shore. If you don't get a strike in a reasonable amount of time, say thirty minutes, try this. Lift your pole and pull your line in an easy sweeping motion so that your bait comes off the bottom and rests about five feet closer and wait. This often produces strikes, I suspect the fish are there but not actively feeding. This action brings them to life.

When using nightcrawlers, the point of the hook always goes through the end of the crawler up to the first barb, then loop the crawler and impale it again up to the end of the hook leaving two to three inches to crawl around.

HEAD

In lakes where there is an abundance of vegetation, such as Lake John and South Delaney Butte, an effective method of using nightcrawlers is to make them float off the bottom with a method C rig. This procedure requires a syringe (purchased at any drugstore or tackle shop) and a knowledge of which is the head and tail sections of the crawler. Crawlers have a band around them at the head section. The method is as follows:

Pull the plunger back on the syringe, fill it full of air, then inject the crawler at or near the band, under their skin, but not through to the innards. The crawler will blow up like a balloon.

Cast this bait out and the crawler will not only float off the bottom, out of the moss, but will wiggle its tail profusely attracting any trout within range.

Another excellent method used to present the crawler as naturally as possible is to thread it internally onto your hook. You need a mini piece of hollow copper tubing and a section of an Aspen branch for a handle. Drill a hole into the Aspen handle, insert the tubing, and you have made a worm threader. It is used as follows:

A. Worm Threader

Center crawler head toward tubing.

HEAD

B.

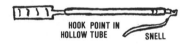

CRAWLER ON THREADER

Carefully thread the crawler through the tubing.

C.

HOOK POINT IN HOLLOW TUBE   SNELL

Place a snelled hook at the exposed hollow tip of the tubing.

D.

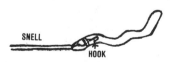

HOOK IN CRAWLER

SNELL

Push the crawler onto the hook. You will find that the hook is completely hidden and that the crawler does not seem to be damaged.

E.

SNELL

HOOK

Final product.

This is an especially effective way to rig crawlers for fishing streams or when trolling.

I have met an extremely successful bait fisherman who uses garlic mini-marshmallows. At first, I "guffawed" this method, but after he caught fish after fish, I chose to get educated. These "mallows" can be purchased in a salmon color ready-made for fishing and are effective because they actually float off the bottom until they dissolve themselves. If you use mallows change them every fifteen minutes or so.

Grasshoppers to trout are as natural a prey as minnows. Sometimes, though, they are very difficult to catch . . . especially if you are at your fishing site. I have seen people chase them down and even injure them with rocks, only to get three or four. Then when these are used up, the chase begins again. Here is a simple and easy method to catch all you want.

Find one of your old fuzzy woolen blankets, have a friend grab an end, then briskly run through the weeds. In one run, you will have all the grasshoppers you want for a days fishing because they stick to the wool blanket with their horney legs.

Crickets are also an excellent bait to use but generally hard to find. Try this, get a loaf of bread, the uncut sourdough variety, cut an end off, then hollow it out so that their is only one entrance. Place it in weeds overnight, then collect the crickets in their trap the next morning. Make sandwiches for your fishing trip with the good portion!

Fishing for lake trout or "Big Macks" (short for Mackinaw) in Colorado is superb in the spring and the fall. For instance, at Grand Lake immediately after ice out, they can easily be caught by trolling, floating, or sinking rapalas all over the lake. This method is of a short duration though because a week or two after ice out the Mack's are primarily caught with sucker meat fished on the bottom.

The method used requires a sliding sinker rig, as described in this chapter and a two hook setup. I suggest using a #2 bait hook for the sucker meat and a #4 or #6 hook for the crawlers. The Mack's will hit both, but the larger fish will primarily take the sucker meat. In Grand Lake, a boat anchored in twenty-five feet of water will net you many Mackinaw strikes. I caution you though to have extreme patience, it is necessary to let this species swallow the bait—that means don't hit at the first tap. Big Mack's like to mouth the bait before it is swallowed. The initial strike of these fish does not indicate to the fishermen the size of the fish, so be sure you use a light drag to avoid breakoffs. That little bite could easily be a twenty-pound Mack mouthing the bait.

By the middle of June, the lake trout have begun to settle into the depths, thus, this method is no longer successful until the fall when the surface waters begin to cool again. During the summer months the lakers are caught trolling 60 to 100 feet deep with lead core line with bait or deep running lures.

At Granby Dam in the spring and fall, Mackinaw or lake trout are often caught that exceed twenty-five pounds in weight by bait fishermen from the bank. The technique is to first catch a sucker on worms, then strip out the meat, then attach it to a method C setup for bottom fishing. Sounds easy, except, that the hook and leader must be woven into the filet. Two techniques will be illustrated. Technique A requires simply weaving the hook into the fillet. Technique B requires the angler to know how to tie a hook on a leader that slides freely on the monofilament leader. Technique B is the preferred method, because it firmly anchors two hooks into the filet and holds it firmly in place. In chapter two, there is an illustration showing you how to professionally snell a hook. If you take this technique a step further, you will be able to develop a specialized leader setup that weaves two hooks into the filet.

TECHNIQUE A

HOOK

LEADER

View of filet

LEADER

Hook & leader through filet

Pull hook and leader through filet, weave in and out of filet, anchor hook into end of filet.

1. How to tie a sliding hook on your leader.

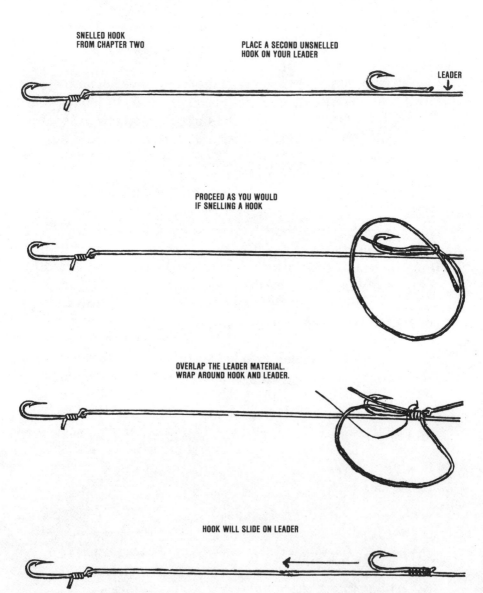

SNELLED HOOK
FROM CHAPTER TWO

PLACE A SECOND UNSNELLED
HOOK ON YOUR LEADER

LEADER

PROCEED AS YOU WOULD
IF SNELLING A HOOK

OVERLAP THE LEADER MATERIAL.
WRAP AROUND HOOK AND LEADER.

HOOK WILL SLIDE ON LEADER

2. How to attach the filet.

First hook

a. Slide second hook up leader and weave first hook into filet, anchor as in the illustration.

Second hook

b. Slide second hook down to leader where the weaving began on hook #1 and anchor into the filet.

Use a four- or six-inch strip of filet and large #2 or #4 hook, weave your hooks into the filet, then cast out as far as you can. Firmly secure your rod, ease off on your drag, and wait until your line starts zinging out, count to five, if you can, and hit the fish.

At this point where the leader attaches to the line, the use of a barrel swivel is necessary. The best knot to use at this juncture is either the improved clench knot or the trilene knot (big fish require good knots).

1. Improved Clench Knot

A.

LINE   SWIVEL   LEADER

B.

Take line through swivel loop, wind around line and put end through first wind. This is a clench knot.

C.

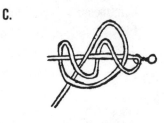

For an improved clench knot, take the terminal end, put it through the single larger circle you have created with the line.

D.

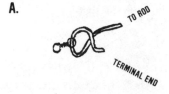

Final Product.

2. Trilene Knot

A.

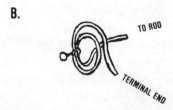

Take line through swivel to form a loop.

B.

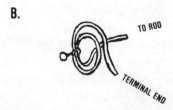

Repeat step A so that your line has gone through the swivel twice.

42

C.

You then wrap the terminal end of the line around your line going to the rod tip (about four times). Note loops A & B.

D.

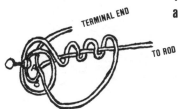

Take the terminal end of your line and put it through loops A & B.

E.

Cinch down by pulling both the terminal end and the line to your rod tip.

I personally prefer the trilene knot, since the monofilament actually grasps the eyelet of the hook with two strands of mono (A & B) instead of one.

The use of floats with bait has always been an excellent method to use when fishing for crappie or blue gill—but is not always as successful when fishing for the deeper suspended cold water fish such as trout. An excellent setup to use to get to these fish is the old sliding bubble trick. Use a bubble, which will allow the line to freewheel through it, attach a three-foot leader and a barrel swivel in the following manner. You will be able to cast great distances and present a bait naturally without the use of a weight.

When you cast this rig out, the bubble, which can be partially filled with water for casting distances, represents a floating weight, while the line and bait slowly cascade through the depths. It looks like this:

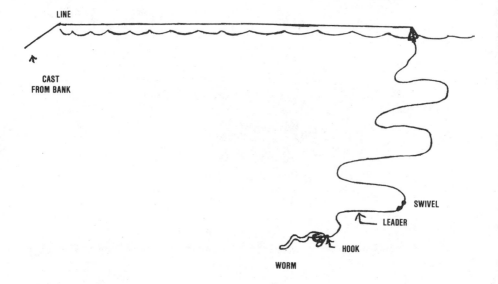

Bait fishing the rivers in Colorado requires a special hookup when fishing the ripples which generally are the most productive areas. Instead of using a bell-shaped sinker in method C, use a pencil-shaped sinker. It allows the bait to stay off the bottom just enough to clear snags, etc. Whenever your bait stops, assume that you have a bite and strike accordingly.

Example:

For fine river fishing with bait, try the Gunnison River, the Taylor River, or the Yampa River. But be sure to check the regulations, some waters are designated as Gold Medal waters which require the use of flies and lures only. Also, be aware that in some of these Gold Medal and Wild Trout waters, the use of hellgramites is allowed as a bait in these waters.

44

In the Eastern United States waters, hellgramites are known as the "carniverous, dark brown, aquatic larva of the Dobson fly." In the Western United States waters, hellgramites are known as the "two-inch, dark brown nymphs of the Stone fly family." They are ugly and crawly, but a dynamite bait and easy to get.

The technique is to find a river, wade out a few feet where a rocky bottom is found, put your net down river from yourself (the net should have a fine screen inserted—nylon works well), and to simply displace rocks with your feet. You will be surprised to find that in ten or fifteen minutes you will have collected a couple of hundred of these one- to three-inch creatures. I usually keep the big ones and throw back the small ones. They can't bite, so be brave, grab one and put it on a hook— this is the most natural bait you can use.

SUGGESTED FISHING AREAS

Lakes	Streams
S. Delaney Buttes	Colorado River
Lake John	Green River
Green Mountain Dam	Yampa River
Left Hand Reservoir	Gunnison River
Shadow Mountain Dam	Frying Pan River
Granby Dam	
Red Dirt Reservoir	
Blue Mesa Reservoir	

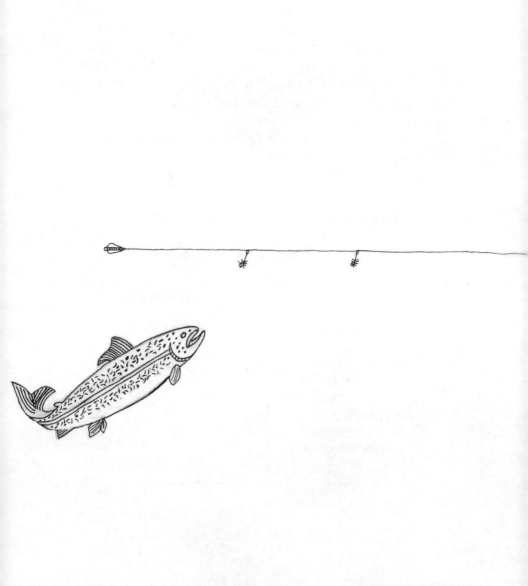

5

Flyfishing with a Spinning Rod

Introduction

Twilight Beckons
the Stars Above

A cool mountain breeze flows down upon the mountains and permeates the forest floor as twilight beckons to the stars approaching. The sounds of a rushing river seem to permeate the air as it casually characterizes this body of water and is only interrupted by the serenades of the owls, ducks, and the buzzing of insects. But what is the sound of the zing-zap-plop, zing-plop that curiously inhabits the inlets and bays of this waterway?

A night fly fisherman—what else? Lake Dillon in the Colorado mountains seems to have spawned a collection of unusual specimens. The typical fisherman who inhabits this realm seeks the shadows of nightfall to avoid laughter by his fellow man and to satisfy his craving for large brown trout. Can you imagine this new breed decked out with chest waders that sag one foot at the crotch (made for professional basketball players), two spinning rods, flashlights, a long handled net, mosquito lotion, and a variety of fly hooks hanging from a fishing vest and to top it off, a portable radio firmly attached to the suspenders of the waders.

Have you ever noticed that fishermen on any given lake usually fish to nightfall and then pack it up until the light of morning? I want to relate a trip that took place at Dillon Reservoir where the fisherman I encountered all stated that "the fishing at this lake is just terrible, it's just not the way it used to be!"

On a Friday afternoon in August, my wife, Mary, packed up the kids, while I packed up the truck for an annual camping outing with about fifteen other families that we were to meet at the lake. An hour and one-half later we arrived at our rendezvous site and began setting up camp. The first order of business was a relaxing dinner and some fellowship. About 6:00 P.M., the guys rustled up about a cord of wood for the campfire while the gals built a fire pit to contain it. As twilight approached, I began to get itchy, knowing that brown trout of immense proportions inhabited this lake.

Cautiously and calmly, I brought up the subject of fishing and generated some interest—but somewhat surprised when no one wanted to join me in this endeavor. Probably because it would be nearly dark by the time we hiked through a tree stand to the lake. So, off I went with my baggy waders and all, while the group generally hee-hawed me. I said to Mary, "Don't worry about me, I'll be back soon!" She knew that meant hours.

As I trod my way through the trees toward the lakeshore, I was surprised to see a four-point buck in velvet. He looked at me as if I was something never seen before. Must have been the portable radio! As I approached the lake, I studied it for several minutes since it was an area I'd never fished before. The lake basically has a mud, sand, and rock bottom except for some bushy shallow bays. Studying the shoreline allowed me to see where a kind of swampy area existed. Tall grass could be seen poking through the water, as well as brush thickets. That was what I was looking for! I carefully trudged forward close to the shoreline into the heart of this bay until I saw a fish dimple the water.

This place was rather awkward, I couldn't put down the other fishing pole on the bank because it was some twenty yards into the marsh, so I stuffed it into my waders—making it look like an antennae. This must have scared the other fishermen away because no others were in sight.

Many years before, my father had taught me the secret of catching large brown trout with spinning gear. The old bubble and fly trick, except that we had a twist! I would guess that well above 95 percent of the fishermen who use this method find their results as less than spectacular, but nevertheless they take some fish. This is simply because they put the fly or flies at the terminal end of the leader. This method sounds good, but consider this—the first thing that passes the fish is the bubble, not the fly. Out of the dozens of fish I caught and released that weekend, only two were caught on an experimental leader added to the end of the bubble. Additionally, all of the fish kept were over two pounds.

The end result to this story was that as I wandered back into camp, it got real quiet, I think I scared them. Anyway, when they saw the unusually large fish I was hefting, they began to question me in detail how I did it.

In the following pages I will detail this procedure by showing how to rig up, what flies to use, and suggest some lakes or reservoirs to try where this method is successful. But first, I want to relate how my father learned this technique.

Many years ago, my father and I went on one of our many weekend fishing excursions and discovered this method really by accident. It all kinda went like this. One of our favorite fishing places in Colorado was Granby Dam. This large impoundment had always been good to us, we consistently caught fish that ranged from ten inches to two pounds by using nightcrawlers and salmon eggs. Back then, as is the case now, Granby had a fine population of large rainbow trout and occasionally, from the bank, we would catch a kokanee salmon on hardware, such as a Super Duper or a Daredevle. Anyway . . .

One Friday afternoon, as we were just about to trek to this favorite impoundment, we were waylaid by a vaporlocked jeep station wagon atop Berthod Pass. That cost us about three hours and the evening fishing that was so good just before dark. We pulled into the Monarch inlet area of Granby Dam at about ten that night and were in the process of setting up our tent when an old fishy smelling critter walked up to us out of the dark. He asked us if we had any extra flashlight batteries. We accommodated him and in that great western fashion, provided him with a cup of coffee from our thermos.

We asked him if he fished any today and he said, "No, fishing at night for large brown trout is best in this lake." He told us that he had just arrived at the lake himself and was preparing to fish when his flashlight gave up the ship.

My dad was real interested in what this old man was talking about and especially in the pictures of five-pound-plus brownies. I wondered about him, he really smelled fishy. Anyway, he told us to come down to the waters edge and he would teach us "a thing or two about the habits of brownies." And off we went!

We hurriedly set up camp, grabbed our rods and bait, then walked to the waters edge, Coleman lantern in hand. He introduced himself as Ed Jano. Old Ed looked at us and our rigs in a strange manner and said, "You two really do need a teachin' about fishin'." He reached into his tackle box and pulled out a little book filled with huge flies and a couple of clear torpedo-shaped casting bubbles and proceeded to cut our lines and "rig us up properly." I thought to myself that this was weird, I'd only used bubbles (the red and white variety for sunfish and crappie and then with a worm, not with huge flies).

It looked something like this. The clear torpedo-shaped bubble was attached to the end of the line and at about eighteen inches up, Ed put a snelled fly (called a Brown Bear) and then about eighteen inches farther up he put another (called a Muddler Minnow). Ed told us that this rig was the key to some very fine fishing and that we would have to set our drags light, cast out as far as we could and then reel in very slow. Actually, he said, "very, very, very slow." So, what had we to lose—I went up the bank and Dad went with Ed.

I think that I must have casted this rig twenty times at least when I heard Ed say, "I had a tech," I think that meant that he had a hit. On the very next cast, as I reeled ultra slow daydreaming or nightdreaming, trying to locate the Big Dipper, my rod nearly was pulled out of my hands. I knew I had one and it was large.

It was about ten minutes later that I finally saw my catch, Ed turned on his flashlight and tried to net brownie, but he had other ideas, and turned tail only to strip out about twenty yards more of my line. Finally, I could feel I was winning the battle as the line came in more easily. Once more, brownie approached the bank, this time for the last time Ed cradled this fish in his net. It was the largest trout that I'd ever caught, a seven-pound eight-ounce brown trout. That night, Dad and I caught a limit each, not one was under four pounds and we had learned a fishing technique that has consistently allowed us to catch large numbers of lunker trout.

Over the years, I have learned some variations to this technique which required me to learn how to tie blood dropper knots, snell flies, and switch to more modern state-of-the-art bubbles. These techniques will all be illustrated in this chapter.

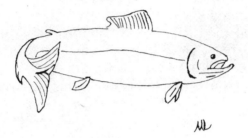

Anyone trout fishing in Colorado can catch a fish on flies either with a flyrod or a spinning rod. A flyrod combination allows the user the advantage of floating lines that keep the fly on top or sinking lines that keep the fly just below the surface. The purist fly fisherman is sure that the use of these combinations is the only way to fly fish. Spinning rods equipped with a bubble and a fly can cover more water and in my opinion catch more fish, at least, in lakes. The natural action of the floating or sinking fly line in a river is another matter—the purist fly fisherman wins hands down.

The flyrod, reel, and line are self-explanatory, but the spinning rod fly outfit isn't. Use no heavier than 8-pound text monofilament, 6-pound is probably the best. Attach a torpedo-shaped clear bubble (float) and one or two flies. Two methods are commonly used by spin fishermen, they are: (1) to attach the bubble about three feet above the fly or (2) to attach the bubble to the terminal end of the line and put a fly three feet above the bubble. Note the following example.

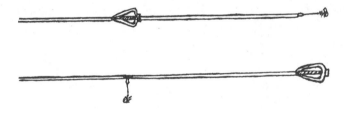

I use both of these methods at once by using a product called "AdjustaBubble." This float allows my line to go through a seated chamber and attach to the line anywhere I want without any knots in my line. It looks something like the following illustration:

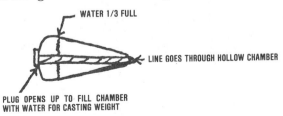

WATER 1/3 FULL

LINE GOES THROUGH HOLLOW CHAMBER

PLUG OPENS UP TO FILL CHAMBER
WITH WATER FOR CASTING WEIGHT

My fly fishing outfit looks like this.

Now for the technique and problem analysis. Which fly do you think catches the most fish? Most people would answer, the bottom fly—but the top fly above the bubble is actually the most productive. The reason, I believe, is because it passes the fish first and is not disturbed by any kind of bubble wake.

The flies used and the time of day on a twenty-four hour clock, directly affect the creel take. For instance, in light hours, I use reasonably small flies such as a female Black Gnat, a Mosquito or a mini Muddler Minnow. If I could only afford three small flies I would use a Black Gnat, Adams and a Renegade. In the darkened hours though, when the moon is not present or very small, I use large flies attached to #2, #4, and #6 hooks. My all-time favorite is the Muddler Minnow, with the Brown Bear, Zonker, Hornberg, and Black Wooley Worm in close contention.

The technique, anytime of the day or night is to cast out as far as you can and retrieve your flies very, very slowly. I always keep my index finger and thumb together around the rod in front of the reel, this allows the line to pass through my fingers, this way I can detect the slightest strike. Patience is the fly fisherman's forte, if you are persistent and don't give up, I guarantee you will put fish on your stringer.

You probably have noticed now that I mentioned flyfishing at night at least twice in the above paragraphs. Flyfishing at night is the only consistent way that I know of catching lunker trout time after time. When fishing at night I am very particular about the way I tie my flies on, I don't just loop them on, but tie a blood dropper. This knot is just about a one hundred percent knot, in other words, my eight-pound test line will not be weakened at the point of the knot. The blood dropper is used to tie a loop into your line above the bubble or below your bubble for a two-fly setup.

Blood Dropper Knot

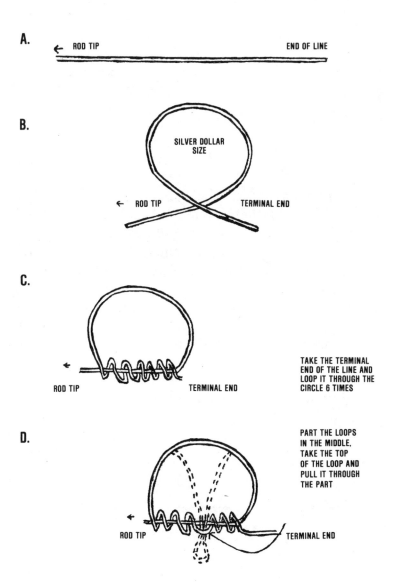

A. ← ROD TIP   END OF LINE

B. SILVER DOLLAR SIZE   ← ROD TIP   TERMINAL END

C. ← ROD TIP   TERMINAL END

TAKE THE TERMINAL END OF THE LINE AND LOOP IT THROUGH THE CIRCLE 6 TIMES

D. ← ROD TIP   TERMINAL END

PART THE LOOPS IN THE MIDDLE, TAKE THE TOP OF THE LOOP AND PULL IT THROUGH THE PART

E.

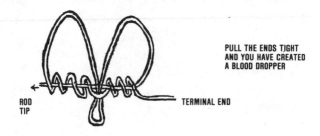

PULL THE ENDS TIGHT
AND YOU HAVE CREATED
A BLOOD DROPPER

ROD
TIP

TERMINAL END

F.

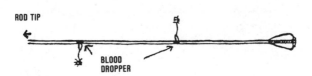

ROD TIP

BLOOD
DROPPER

Another advantage to this knot is that it sits straight out from the monofilament and does not parallel the line up or down, thus, your fly tends to stay away from tangles on your line. Now for the fly.

Buying snelled flies used to be no problem in Colorado—they were always available—not now though, I have seen very few in the last ten years. So, now we must snell our own and this is how. Use twelve-pound test line for the snell, it is rigid enough to stay away from your line and avoids tangles. Simply tie an improved clench knot on the eye of the fly and then tie it or loop it onto your blood dropper.

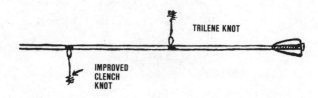

TRILENE KNOT

IMPROVED
CLENCH
KNOT

Another excellent knot to use to snell flies is the trilene knot.* It is probably superior in strength to the improved clench knot and is easy to tie.

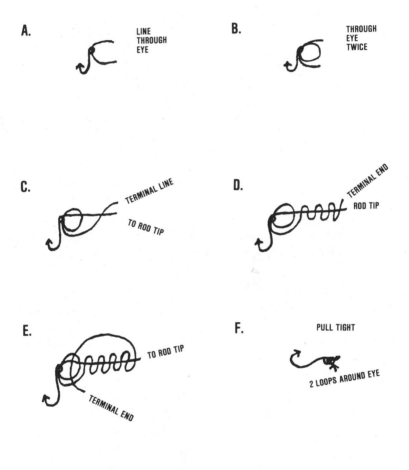

A. LINE THROUGH EYE

B. THROUGH EYE TWICE

C. TERMINAL LINE TO ROD TIP

D. TERMINAL END ROD TIP

E. TO ROD TIP TERMINAL END

F. PULL TIGHT 2 LOOPS AROUND EYE

*SEE CHAPTER IV FOR A DETAILED TRILENE KNOT.

Note that if you choose to loop your fly onto your blood dropper, you need to put the line loop through your snelled hook loop to create a square knot. Doing it any other way will weaken this conjunction.

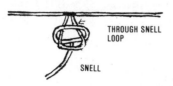

THROUGH SNELL
LOOP

SNELL

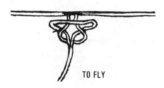

TO FLY

When you try night fishing in this manner, I suggest
you try the area at Dillon Dam, near Frisco where the
Blue River runs into the Dam. You will need waiders and
a good flashlight, cast into this area just where the
current seems to end and it becomes calmer. Crank ever
so slowly and be patient. I have often thrown flies for
over ninety minutes without a strike and then gotten
strikes every cast after that for hours.

After trying this technique for a period of time, keep
a mental note or a log on the numbers of fish caught
above and below the bubble. You will note, very quickly,
that the scales are tipped far forward toward those flies
above the bubble. For several years now, my bubble
resides at the terminal end of my line and my flies are
arranged upward toward my rod tip. This is the
recommended method to use for success!

One thing to remember about night fishing with flies
is that when the moon is out and bright upon the water—
go to bed and rest, the fish just don't hit flies. Also, do not
take a lantern near the water, especially at the waters
edge, it spooks the fish and severely limits your success.
Shield it from the water and place it far onto the bank.

Another extremely effective method of fishing a
river with flies and a spinning rod is to set your rig up as
you would for night fishing with the bubble at the
terminal end of your line. Fill the bubble completely full

and cast upstream into the most turbulent water and reel in just fast enough to keep a tight line. Try to keep the bubble and flies where you will know the drift will cross into a deep hole or behind a rock. You will once again be amazed at the success achieved. I generally use a #6 Silver Zonker and a #6 Black Wooley Worm with a red tail.

Turbulent areas of white water or fast running deep water is generally fished little because most people feel it is just too tough to fish. This kind of water is filled to the brim with lunkers.

On a recent trip to the Bighorn National Recreation Area, I had the opportunity to fish the Bighorn River. It is rated among the ten top trout streams in all North America and from my point of view is justly rated. The large rainbow and brown trout readily took our flies. The average fish generally exceed three pounds and ten-pounders are quite common.

You might be wondering by now what this has to do with fishing in Colorado? This trip was proof that you are never too old to learn new techniques. The water of the Bighorn moves very fast and, thus, the locals have devised a fishing method, utilizing flies and a spinning rod that really works.

The technique is to attach a beaded keel sinker to about a three-foot leader and attach a large fly to the end. Cast upstream at about a forty-five degree angle and allow your line to drift down river while slowly retrieving. I know of numerous places in Colorado where swift water is the rule and fishing pressure is practically nil because of these conditions. Try this technique in swift water areas such as the Eagle River or Gore Canyon area of the Colorado River.

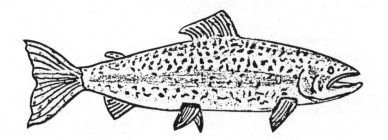

Try these impoundments:

Lakes

North Delaney Buttes—16-inch minimum length brown
   trout
Dillon Reservoir—at the Blue River inlet
Green Mountain Dam—at the Blue River inlet
Round/Percy lakes—4 mile walk (all brookies—atop
   Rabbit Ears Pass)
Granby Dam
Blue Mesa Reservoir

Rivers

Colorado River
Eagle River
Taylor River
Platte River
Gunnison River
Blue River

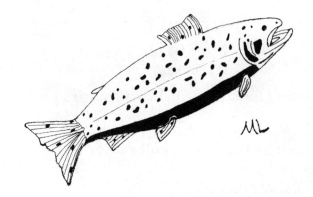

6

Flyfishing with a Fly Rod

Introduction

The use of a fly rod, reel, and line by the general angler is often seen as difficult and appropriate only for the "expert" angler. Flyfishing, as in all methods, is a means to an end—catching fish. If you speak with the purist fly fisherman (one that fishes only in this manner), he or she will confuse and befuddle your mind with double-tapered fly lines, tapered monofilament leaders, floating lines, and the like. The well-rounded fisherman, that is, one who utilizes all manners of fishing, uses the fly rod as one of many productive methods in their arsenal.

I clearly remember my first experience with a sort-of-fly rod, it was in June 1954. At the crack of dawn, my fishing pal, John Johnson and I, jumped on our bikes, fishing gear and all, and began our trek to the Golden fishing pond. It was the site of the first annual fishing derby for us young'uns.

We had been watching this lake for over a week, ever since it was stocked. From the trees overlooking the lake, literally hundreds of trout could be seen awaiting the derby. We arrived several hours early to assure our position near the tree. Our plan was simple. One of us would watch the fish from the tree and direct the other in a casting effort. After seemingly hours of waiting, 8:00 A.M. finally arrived—the derby was about to begin.

John and I used salmon eggs to catch two fish each very quickly, until the derby people told us we couldn't climb the tree anymore. Thus, our method of attack and success was threatened. Also, about three hundred kids completely encircled this small lake, making movement difficult. As the hours mounted, our patience wained and fish panicked avoiding anything that hit the water.

Over the years, my fishing style hasn't really changed that much, in that I had brought spinning equipment, lots of tackle, and two extra poles to be used when one tangled up. One of the three rods was a metal nine-foot telescoping fly rod with a fly reel, line and all. About seven that night, I told John to hold our spot—I was going to try the fly at the other end of the lake.

I remember pulling out line and getting the fly probably ten feet out into the lake, then pulling it back in. On my second cast, I caught a stocker rainbow on this fly. My excitement was as incredible as my ego! Before the days end, I had caught five fish (my limit), two on salmon eggs and three on flies. But more importantly, I had added a new dimension to my fishing skills.

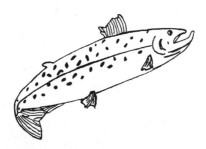

ML

The initial cost of your equipment most probably will be higher than comparable spinning gear, but it will generally be more maintenance free and last longer. Fly reels are simple. They are designed to hold a special type of line which can be pulled out and reeled in. The rods are long and flexible, generally eight to twelve feet in length, to allow one to cast modest distances. Now, with the equipment in mind, it is necessary to select the proper line to match the fly rod and reel combination.

There are several types of fly lines available which are identified as follows:

A. Double taper (DT) lines have a long level consistent section in the middle and are tapered at each end. When this line begins to wear, simply reverse it.

B. Level lines (L) are of a consistent diameter throughout its length.

C. Weight forward lines (WF) are weighted on the terminal end, so that more distance can be achieved in casting.

D. Shooting taper lines (ST) are somewhat unique and specialized, they are attached to a monofilament backing and can be casted long distances.

All of these lines are floating, sinking, or floating and sinking, thus, you must choose whether you wish to fish on the top or below the surface. A good choice for the novice is a double-taper floating/sinking line where initially the fly floats, but will sink the longer it's left in the water. Leaders and how to attach them to your fly line are another issue.

The two most popular leaders are the tapered leader or a level monofilament leader, which maintains a specific pound test throughout its length. I would recommend a tapered leader for the beginner, since it allows for a longer smoother cast.

Attaching a leader to a fly line is of paramount importance because it can negate many of the positives of good equipment—knots tend to weigh down the leader at the point of conjunction. Standard fishing knots, like the blood knot, are not efficient when tying two different types of leaders together with different diameters. One that is fairly easy to tie and illustrate is as follows, it is called the nail knot.

A. Place a large needle between your fly line and connecting monofilament.

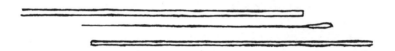

B. Wrap monofilament around fly line and needle.

C. Thread needle with the monofilament as shown.

D. Pull needle through and pull the leader tight. The finished product will be neat and strong.

The choice of your fly rod hinges on the choice of your line, that is, fly lines come in numerous diameters and must match the rod for efficiency. This problem is solved by the manufacturers—on each rod, the most efficient line diameter is identified on the rod label. Choose your rod as you would any other item, quality and comfort. My favorite fly rod is an eleven-foot custom graphite model that feels good to me. Other anglers may feel comfortable with lengths of eight and one-half to ten feet. When in doubt, go to one of the many specialty flyfishing shops within any metropolitan area.

Flies, like the rod, reel, line, and leader are a personal choice. My favorites will be annotated throughout the rest of this text. Flies come in several categories as follows:

A. Wet flies resemble drowned adult insects, bait fish, or insects just hatching. They are fished just below the surface. An example of this type of fly is the Black Gnat with a red tail.

B. Dry flies imitate adult forms of insects that land on the water surface, thus, they are fished directly on the surface. An example is the Mayfly.

C. Nymphs imitate underwater larvae of insects. These flies are fished below the surface near or on the bottom. An example of this is the Hare's Ear.

D. Streamers imitate bait fish and can be fished both on the top and below the surface. Surface streamers that are my personal favorites are the Zonker and the Muddler Minnow. A subsurface streamer (weighted in the fly) is the Wooley Bugger.

You will find that some patterns simply work better than others, I would recommend that you start with patterns that are known consistent producers, such as the Black Gnat with a red tail, size #12 or a small size #10 Muddler Minnow. Attach these flies to the terminal end of your leader by the use of a trilene knot.

If this is your first outing with a flyfishing outfit then you should assure that conditions are right. That is, make sure that the streams are low and clear and don't use this method if a rain storm has just muddied the waters. Fishing during a rain storm is excellent though. Lake fishing with a fly rod is excellent at Green Mountain Dam where the Blue River first enters it. Your chances of success are multiplied when adverse weather conditions do not muddy the water.

Once at a lake or stream, pull out several yards of line and begin to gently cast with your wrist, not your whole arm, until you have ten to twenty yards of line out. It is not necessary to go for distance, many times fish are within five to ten feet of the shore, especially in the spring and fall. To retrieve the line simply reach out and pull two to three feet smoothly toward your hand holding the rod and reel—then grab it (with the rod and reel hand) between your forefinger and thumb, continue in this manner until you are ready for another cast.

In streams, it is necessary to fish directly above the ripples and allow your fly to float through the ripples and settle into pockets where the fish are concentrated. Any momentary pause of the fly action probably indicates a strike, so strike accordingly. You will quickly develop your own technique, so experiment a bit on slow retrieves, fast retrieves, and even allowing your fly to float down the current before a retrieve.

There are some nifty little tricks that you can do with a fly rod, reel, and line that just can't be done with other outfits. For instance, have you ever fished within a river where a great ripple and subsequent pool existed but you just could not cast because of the foliage? Next time this happens, pull out your fly line and float it down this ripple, disregarding any kind of cast, then spin your rod in a circular motion upstream. You will find that the fly line is lifted off the surface and can be accurately cast upriver in this manner. The line is actually spiraled upriver in a controlled manner and exactly where you want it.

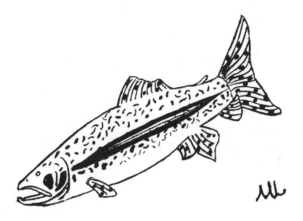

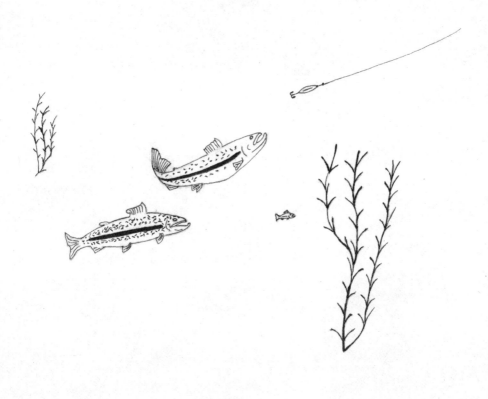

7

Fishing with Artificial Lures

Introduction

An aura of mystery and intrigue permeates the earth, as a raging inferno of volcanic action uplifts and downshifts into the earth, creating a monolith, which then gives way to a seemingly unending cool artic front that gnaws and tears at its seams. As this creation gives way to glacial action and eventual stability, the Rocky Mountains and the State of Colorado are born. Majestic is the beauty of Colorado, with its peaks, stands of pines, aspen, high moutain meadows, lakes, streams, and abundant wild life.

It was the fourth Thursday, after the third Friday in September that these thoughts went through my mind. It was nearly five o'clock in the morning. Old Ron and I were in the midst of a contest—a fishing contest in which I knew I would need all the help I could to win. Ron was so good with a fly that he could set a bucket on the lake shore, put a fly in it, and the fish would jump out of the lake into the bucket. He is the typical, dyed-in-the-wool, fly fisherman who always caught fish. On the other hand, my techniques included a bit of everything, which is the reason that I often carry numerous rods, each set up for any occasion.

We were at a lake, which has no name, but is accurately located within a fifty mile radius of Topanas. Several years ago, my Dad dubbed it "Lunker Lake." This small fifteen-acre lake was incredible, seething with aquatic life in which many very large trout inhabited. The smallest trout caught out of this lake, over the last few years, was an eighteen-inch brookie.

The scene in the camper was chaotic, both of us trying to beat each other to the lakeshore—knowing that this last day of our annual archery hunting trip would be spent fishing here.

Ron weighed about two-hundred and fifty pounds and he took full advantage of every opportunity to outfox me when it came to fishing or hunting. As he heard the alarm ring and saw me already dressing, he slowly dragged out of his sleeping bag laughing. He had gone to sleep with his fly vest and waiders on! Needless to say, I was still straining to get my chest waiders on when he left the camper chuckling.

I could see Ron casting to a rise as I approached the lakeshore, what I couldn't see was the twenty-inch rainbow on his stringer. Knowing it would be hard to catch him, I began to fish in earnest—the first of the four rods I brought with me was a twelve-foot split bamboo fly rod ready to go. On the first cast of the day, the fly gently rested on the surface, only to be engulfed into a cavernous mouth. My reaction was, "I got one, Ron, I got one!" Actually, it got me because the run was so quick and ferocious, the fish immediately stripped the line off the reel and left me speechless. So much for fishing with my fly rod! Next, I tried flies and a bubble, then drowned nightcrawlers and salmon eggs, only to see Ron catch his third fish of the day—this time a twenty-four-inch cutthroat.

Eventually, because of the tangles or broken line on snags, I was down to one usable rod in which the line and reel were hopelessly snarled. But with some patience, it would be usable. I freed about twenty yards of monofilament, then decided that a large spoon would be the ticket to freeing the rest of the line. Now the lake was chock full of moss—and lures just couldn't be used effectively here. So, I thought I would cast it out and reel in so quickly that it would stay on top and "zowie," my line would be untangled.

As I cast, the lure sailed thirty yards into the lake. I began to waterski it back when I noticed the large wake behind it that quickly became the back of a huge "hawg" trout. Wow! I knew it was going to hit. And hit it did. This fish made run after run, in and out of the moss, taking huge amounts of line each time. Finally, I gained a few inches, feet, and then yards. When this fish came into view, I couldn't believe its size, it looked like at least three feet. Its last run tensed my senses, I knew that a jump or the lack of keeping a tight line might be the end of this battle. As I coaxed this behemoth into my net, it finally dawned on me that I really got him. The rainbow measured twenty-seven and one-half inches and weighed eight pounds-nine ounces.

On this outing Ron caught five fish and I caught six (all on lures), the smallest fish was eighteen inches and the largest, my twenty-seven and one-half-incher. The moral of the story is that I used to use lures as a last resort, now I use them often, when conditions seem right. The following text will be oriented toward spinners, lures, and spoons. It is intended to strengthen your knowledge of their use and significantly increase your creel take.

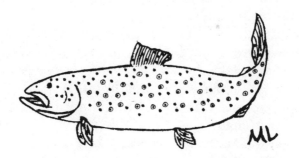

LURES

Fishing with lures seems pretty much self-explanatory, you put them on, throw them out, and reel them in. It's really not that simple though if you are to match the water to a lure, that is, what type of lure is appropriate to the various water conditions?

Lures are an important part of anyone's fishing arsenal, but with all the varieties on the market today, which ones seem to work the best? There are spinners, spinner baits, crank baits, stick baits, buzz baits, minnow plugs, spoons, etc. In Colorado, minnow plugs, spinners, and spoons are the rule for trout.

Spinners have revolving blades that turn around a shaft to imitate minnows. They are extremely effective in the shallows and ripples of streams or the shallow inlets and bays of reservoirs. A ball bearing swivel is necessary when attaching a spinner to your line to avoid excessive line twist.

Minnow plugs generally float at the surface until retrieved, then they may sink or stay on the surface. These plugs generally have extremely good action however fished and imitate minnows. The use of a swivel on these baits often inhibits the action of the lure, therefore, attach them directly to your line.

Spoons often imitate wounded bait fish or a variety of minnows. They are made to cast distances, thus, you will find them in a variety of thicknesses. Always use a swivel on spoons, their motion will often severely twist your line.

Spinner type lures are probably the most effective in streams where short casting distances are generally the rule and light lures are preferred to avoid snags. It is necessary to "read" the water in streams or rivers to be productive. In the spring, summer, and fall, seek the ripples, above and below pools, this is where the majority of trout lie. Cast in a forty-five degree angle upstream and retrieve slowly—keeping only enough tension on the line to keep the lure working and to avoid snags. Strikes usually occur in the ripples, just as they give way to pools or as they go into undercut banks. In winter, you will find favorite ripples devoid of fish, this is due to the phenomena of the water, as discussed in chapter three. The fish will be found at this time of the year in the deep pools near the bottom.

In large lakes and reservoirs, spoons are often used to cast from shallow bays into deeper water where distance is a factor. If fishing in water that is reasonably deep, such as Granby Dam, one can actually count down a spoon. That is, cast it out, once the spoon hits the water, count from one to ten, then reel in smoothly. If no strike occurs in two or three casts, then on the next cast, count down to nine, then eight, then seven, etc. When you get a strike, you will know where the fish are suspended. So, if you get a strike at seven, then count down to seven each time before you start your retrieve.

If the fish are rising, try to throw to the rises, this often produces an immediate strike. When they are not rising, cover as much water as possible by casting in a 180 degree half circle from the bank. If you don't catch a fish in a reasonable length of time, move on and continue this procedure until you catch a fish.

Minnow plugs generally cannot be cast long distances and are somewhat a specialty item. Their primary use is in shallow bays where water enters reservoirs, such as the Blue River inlet at Dillon Dam. The technique is to cast the plug out and to retrieve it in water that is moving. The speed can be varied to imitate an injured fish, this technique is especially effective at night when no moon is visible.

If you have a boat, troll with hardware. Hardware comes in many shapes and sizes, but generally is about three feet long with a rudder at one end and blades attached to a steel cable, it has no hooks, so you must add leader material and attach a lure or a nightcrawler to the end. To the fish it looks like a school of small bait fish.

Lake John near Walden is a great place to go just after ice out, the fish generally average about two pounds, but six- to eight-pounders are not at all uncommon. Granby Dam is generally good year round for this type of trolling. But, beware, use improved clench knots or the trilene knot because lake trout of twenty-plus pounds are common at this impoundment. Hardware is extremely effective in all large lakes within the state, it also offers some diversity, in that, a lure or bait is attached with a leader to the terminal end of the tackle. This method is the principle way that kokanee salmon are caught by anglers.

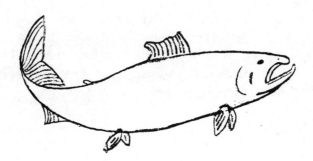

Addendum One
Kokanee Salmon

Kokanee salmon are a landlocked Pacific sockeye salmon which are stocked into our large impoundments by the Colorado Fish and Game Division annually. Like most typical salmon they have a four year life cycle. The culmination of their life ends in the fall of the year when they begin to amass in untold numbers and seek the rivers that flow into these impoundments to spawn. The kokanee does not reproduce well in landlocked waters and thus is unable to sustain its own population. So, the Colorado Department of Fish and Wildlife closes off some specific salmon spawning areas to fishing each year to collect the spawn and artificially hatch them for the states' following year stocking schedule.

In the meantime, the state waters containing these fish are open to snagging. One of the first waters to open for this season is Green Mountain Reservoir on September 1, the rest open October 1, of each year. But kokanee snagging regulations do change so check the regulations before you fish.

The setup for this type of fishing is generally a #4 treble hook with a lead filled shank. During the peaks of the run (October-November) there are literally thousands of them congregated and concentrated in and around the inlet areas. There are so many that you can cast a snag hook out and often snag one each cast.

Sounds easy, but there actually is a specific technique. If you were to travel to Green Mountain Reservoir, for instance, you would see people lined up on the shore casting and snagging and casting and snagging. You would also notice that some of these "snaggers" seem to be catching about ninety percent of the fish. The reason is that snagging requires a technique just like any other form of fishing.

The technique is as follows; cast out as far as you can and allow your hook to settle to the bottom (where the snags are), quickly take up the slack and pull the line hard, reel up the slack, allow it to sink to the bottom, pull again, etc. This keeps the hook on the bottom where the fish are. Many unsuccessful snaggers throw out where the fish are but don't allow their hook to sink to the bottom before each successive snag—thus, no fish or few fish are on their stringers.

Bait shops love this season, there is a logical reason for this though, it is financial, the snag hooks cost twenty-five to fifty cents each, depending whether you get them in town or the mountain sport shops. I never take less than a half gross of these hooks on each trip. Fear not though, with a coleman stove, an eight dollar lead melting pot and twelve dollar snag hook mold you can make them yourself for less than ten cents each. Two outings will more than pay for your pot and mold. I get my lead from junkyards and sometimes from tire shops (when they are willing to part with it). In my garage, I can pour one gross of hooks per hour and I use only one three-hook mold.

At spawning time, the fish average sixteen to twenty inches each and generally weigh around two pounds. The current limit is forty per day with forty in possession.

During the non-snagging season, the limit is ten in possession. In the spring time trollers are extremely successful in their attempts to catch these fish on pop-gear and a worm trailer or small lure. Williams Fork

Reservoir, after ice out, is superb.

Unknown to many fishermen is the fact that kokanee can be caught in good numbers with flies, (and bubble) while fishing for trout. I have only caught them at night this way—but they were caught in numbers. One of the best spots is where the Ten Mile River inlet empties into Dillon Dam.

Addendum Two
Wintertime Fishing

Usually about the end of January, I can stand it no longer. I have even begun to see fish in my dreams. Of course, all of the lakes are iced up by now and finally safe to walk on (but check carefully!). Ice fishing rigs look like they are made for "hobbits," they are only a foot to eighteen inches long, contain a simple primitive reel, and the tips are as small as wire. This is because in the wintertime the fish are sluggish and they don't react the same way as they do in the open water months. This wee tip is needed to see the strikes, the smallest little bob could mean one of the largest fish you have ever seen.

You need an ice auger or a chipping device such as a mountain climbers pick or axe to make a hole. Do not make it big enough for a person to go through, because after you are gone another fisherman may wander by a day or two later and fall through. An eight- to ten-inch circular hole is adequate. Use worms, eggs, or tiny jugs for ice fishing. Let them go to the bottom and then pull them up a foot or two every few minutes until you find the fish.

One of the best places to ice fish is Turquoise Lake near Leadville. You will generally only catch cutthroats but they certainly are willing. You might also catch a big lake trout that won't fit through the hole.

One of my favorite winter fishing places is at Shadow Mountain Dam where the water is pumped through the canal from Granby into Shadow Mountain. This area of water is open year round and offers some really excellent fishing by conventional methods, if you can stand the cold.

Wintertime river fishing is also very different from the other times of the year. The usual ripples that are fished successfully in the spring, summer, and fall are not productive in the winter. Concentrate on the pools, this is where the trout congregate in the winter months.

Addendum Three
Other Species of Fish

This addendum will be devoted to a discussion about some other species of fish and where they can be found in large numbers.

In Colorado near the Kansas border there is a place called Bonnie Dam. The catch here is a mixture of nearly all warm water species—but in the months of April and May something special happens, the walleye pike and white bass are on the bite. The walleye's average around three pounds each and the white bass, a couple pounds each. The technique is to use a lead headed jig, preferably a Sassy Shiner or a Sassy Shad. Cast it out from the bank or from a boat and retrieve as quickly as you would a lure.

A new species of fish just introduced into these waters a couple of years ago is called the "Wybrid." They are a cross between a striped bass and a white bass. The Colorado Department of Wildlife estimates that they have the potential to reach a weight of ten pounds. This year they are expected to be in the four- to six-pound range. In these waters, I use an open-face reel spooled with ten-pound test line with an adjustable drag on my reel.

Did you realize that Colorado now ranks as one of the best fishing spots for northern pike? Eleven Mile Reservoir near St. George is probably the best place to go. Fish the shallows in late spring and early summer with large flies or lures and be prepared—twenty-pounders are very common. For this species you will need to use about a six-inch steel leader to assure that this toothy critter doesn't break your line. Be sure that you *do not* put your finger in their mouths, their teeth are razor sharp on both sides. Use a large net, a gaff or a club (a half a tree trunk will probably do nicely).

At Pueblo Reservoir, down in the Southern part of our state, you will be pleased to know that it houses monster catfish. On one outing alone last year, our party brought back forty, averaging about thirty inches each. Our technique is to fish near the inlet with minnows purchased at the local bait shop. We use a sliding sinker rig, open-face reels that house a couple hundred yards of twenty-pound test monofilament. Cast out as far as you can, then wait and watch, it won't be long until you get one. Channel catfish are some of the best eating around. Fish at night for lunkers, in the daytime the bite seems to fall off and the fish are much smaller.

In March my family goes on our annual trek to Lake Powell, also known as Glen Canyon Dam. A boat is not a necessity but it is highly recommended. They can be rented cheaply at any of the many marinas. The fish we seek are the striped bass, the landlocked variety. On our trip last year, our combined catch (three families) was forty-one stripers for two days of fishing, the smallest fish was eight pounds.

The technique is to use a pole comparable to a surf casting rig and a reel such as the Mitchell 300 or better yet the 302. Spool it with a twenty-pound test line. I have an eighteen-foot boat equipped with a Lawrence Fish-LOC-A-TOR. If you don't have a depth finder, fear not, just motor up to where all the boats are.

The method used to catch these fish is simple. Use the bait sliding sinker rig with about a three-foot leader, attach this to a large hook (which has about a four-inch shank and double hooks and cast it out. No one anchors, you simply drift across the channel, then go back across and do it again and again. Last year we caught them at about the thirty- to thirty-five-foot level consistently. Be sure not to allow your bait to sink below this level, the thermocline level, at this time of year, in this particular lake, is between fifteen and thirty-five feet. Total depth ranged from thirty-five to one hundred-fifteen feet.

The area to fish is the Wahweap Marina area close to Page, Arizona, or the closer Bull Frog Marina area of the lake in the heart of Utah. I prefer Wahweap, primarily because it offers many family diversions—it houses a major National Park Service visitor center which provides the visitor with historical information about the dam itself. Also, the area is rich in the culture of the American Indian.

Farthest West is one of the most fabulous fishing areas in North America. The prey is the American white sturgeon that inhabit these waters. The limit is one fish and the minimum length is forty inches—that's three feet, four inches. My last keeper sturgeon weighed one hundred fifty-five pounds and was over seven feet long.

The white sturgeon has no internal bones, only cartilage, the bones of this prehistoric fish are external in the form of heavy sharp diamond-shaped plates prevalent on its body. This prehistoric fish has a mouth like a vacuum cleaner, it eats native grass shrimp, mussels, and soft shelled clams.

The place to catch these critters, often called

"diamond backs" by the locals, is San Pablo Bay, which is surrounded on one side by the city of Vallejo, the old Hamilton Air Force Base, Rodeo, and Upper San Francisco Bay. The best place to fish is near Hamilton Air Force Base close to a structure called, "The Pump House," or near bouy number four.

If you employ your own boat, a compass is a necessity. In the early morning hours the fog often allows vision to only a few yards. The best way to fish for these denizens of the deep is to charter a fishing boat at Rodeo Marina or Dowlrelios. A full day charter will cost about sixteen dollars, rods and bait are extra—but the whole trip will cost you less than twenty dollars per day.

A sliding sinker rig is used in conjunction with a three-foot steel leader. The size of the sinker ranges from three to eight ounces depending on the tide. The bait used is live grass shrimp and can be purchased at local bait stores in increments of one-fourth pound. I use a custom made rod that is similar to a surf rod and a level wind Penn Squidder reel that holds about four hundred yards of thirty-pound test quality line. It is necessary that you learn to cast this type of reel. Cast your bait out and just wait.

The wait won't be long because the sculpin fish (locally called bullheads), flounder, striped bass (up to fifty pounds), croakers and an occasional sand shark will keep you busy. You can *always* tell a sturgeon bite, it is not the kind of jolting bite that the striper provides, nor the pecking of the other species, but simply a short steady movement of the rod tip that dips about three inches. Be ready, you will only get about two of these dips, grab your pole, be sure of a reasonably loose drag and set the hook hard.

The experience of fishing for this species will last you a lifetime. I have probably caught at least ten sturgeon over seventy-five pounds. The world rod and reel record for sturgeon has been broken in the large tributaries that feed these bays (Sacramento/San Juaquin river systems). Best fishing seasons are December through March.

Another spectacular area to fish is the Florida Keys. Charter boats are the rule, the costs range from $150 to $200 per day, but split between five or six, it really is quite reasonable. The best starting point is Garrison Bite, located on the gulf side of the city of Key West, Florida. Retired military personnel may be able to charter the Naval hospital's boat for around twenty dollars per day.

The species fished for range from sail fish, white marlin, dolphin fish (not the mammal), cobia, tarpin, Spanish mackeral, weakfish (sea trout), red snapper and last but not least the "Jew fish" as the locals call it. It is actually a variety of giant groupers (the last one I caught was 240 pounds, not large by their standards, but adequate).

You use a Penn Squidder level wind type of reel, a heavy rod and troll with a fish called balahoo for the more exotic species. You still fish with cut bait, usually sardines for the other species. For large groupers, a thirty-pound mackeral and a sturdy hook, half as long as your arm is preferred.

About the Author

Mert Leeper has roamed the wilds of Colorado ever since he was able to walk. Not only is he an avid fisherman, but an accomplished archery and gun hunter. He has authored a published magazine article called "Hunting the High Country," which deals with archery hunting, and taught Colorado trout fishing classes for the last several years. His unique style of writing and knowledge of the out-of-doors makes this book one that should be in the library of each person who fishes in Colorado.

Index

Log

DATE	PLACE	FISH	WEIGHT	MOON CYCLE

DATE	PLACE	FISH	WEIGHT	MOON CYCLE

DATE	PLACE	FISH	WEIGHT	MOON CYCLE